Sales is a Contact Sport

Copyright © 2020 By Keith Baulsir

All rights reserved

YOUR RIGHTS: This book is restricted to your personal use only. It does not come with any other rights.

LEGAL DISCLAIMER: This book is protected by international copyright law and may not be copied, reproduced, given away, or used to create derivative works without the publisher's expressed permission. The author retains full copyrights to this book.

The author has made every reasonable effort to be as accurate and complete as possible in the creation of this book and to ensure that the information provided is free from errors; however, the author/publisher/reseller assumes no responsibility for errors, omissions, or contrary interpretation of the subject matter herein and does not warrant or represent at any time that the contents within are accurate due to the rapidly changing nature of the Internet.

Any perceived slights of specific persons, peoples, or organizations are unintentional.

The purpose of this book is to educate and there are no guarantees of income, sales or results implied. The publisher/author/reseller can therefore not be held accountable for any poor results you may attain when implementing the techniques or when following any guidelines set out for you in this book.

SALES IS A CONTACT SPORT

Sales is a Contact Sport

Table of Contents:

Introduction

About Me

Attitude Comes First

Sales Behaviors & Behavior Tracking

Prospecting Tips

Outreach Examples

Meeting Preparation Like a Mad Scientist

How to Run a Meeting

Pitching & Following Up

Conclusion

Introduction

There is nothing quite like sales. It's a blend of art and science, and closing a big deal can give you one of the happiest and most exhilarating feelings in the world. Sales success can provide an adrenalin rush like few other jobs, and it can also be very lucrative. On top of that, it's also a great way to help people and if you're great at sales and you learn to listen to your clients and provide solutions that truly benefit them, your clients will become some of your closest friends. With that being said, it is also a very challenging profession with a lot of pitfalls. After more than a decade of success in sales in the cutthroat sports & entertainment industry, I decided to write this book to teach anyone how to become successful in this profession. If you follow the steps outlined in the book I am confident that you will become an extremely productive salesperson.

Even if you're not a salesman or saleswoman, you can also use these skills in other areas of your life. Sales is based on communication, and being good at sales will help you with your side hustle, it will help you with dating, and it will help you with relationships with friends and family.

I will never forget when I was in my early 20's and first getting started in the sports industry and closed my first "big" deal. In retrospect, it wasn't a huge deal but I didn't know that at the time and it was one of the happiest and proudest moments of my life. The joy and pride weren't about the money (I wasn't making much), they stemmed from a sense of accomplishment that I felt after grinding for months chasing the deal. Working in sales is a roller coaster because it has big ups like that, and it also has very big downs. It can be completely devastating when you lose a deal you've worked really hard on. You face rejection every single day in sales, and some people will be downright obnoxious and mean to you. People will even disappear and "ghost" you for no apparent reason, and some will even lie to your face. People think they can lie to salespeople because they think salespeople are shady. There are plenty of honest salespeople, but that is the perception in our industry so you'll need rock-solid sales skills to overcome it. Think of what comes to mind when someone says "used car salesman" and that is the perception we need to overcome.

In this business there's a saying that "you eat what you kill." The word eat doesn't just symbolize surviving and putting food on the table for yourself and your family, to me it symbolizes living a good life. Your ability to "eat" and live a good, fruitful life is directly tied to your ability to close deals. It may sound drastic, but if you can't close deals you won't last very long in this profession. One of my favorite TV shows of all time is Mad Men which is about an advertising agency in New York City in the 1960's. On the show, Don Draper (the main character – an extremely successful/legendary ad executive) alludes to "you eat what you kill" when he tells one of his employees that "bringing in business is the key to your salary, your status, and your self-worth." It's undisputed that you either sink or swim in this profession, and this book is going to teach you how to swim like a fish.

Mad Men's Don Draper

On the bright side, if you're good and you're a top producer, sales can be the highest paid profession in the world. I'll illustrate this with some data from US News & World Report. According to their annual labor study, the highest paid profession in America in 2019 was Anesthesiologist and it paid $265,990 per year. The second-highest paid profession was Surgeon at $251,890. To become an Anesthesiologist, you need a 4-year college degree, a 4-year degree from medical school, and a 2-year residency. That's 10-years and hundreds of thousands of dollars in tuition (or millions) before you ever make $265K per year. Most people start college at about 18 or 19, meaning an Anesthesiologist will be about 30 years old before they finally start making the big bucks. And even when they start working, they'll be buried in debt for years while they pay off their education. Becoming a Surgeon is even worse because you need 4-years of college and 4-years of medical school, and most surgeons need a 4-year residency before they make it big. Don't get me wrong, a Surgeon plays a very important role in society and they help keep us all healthy, but my point is that a successful salesman or saleswoman can make much more than an Anesthesiologist or a Surgeon. While it's rare, some salesmen and saleswomen make 7-figures per year, and many sales jobs don't even require a bachelor's degree. It's a great profession because it doesn't have the elevated barriers to entry that other high-earning jobs require, and it has the same (or better) earning potential. Plus, as I mentioned at the beginning of this chapter, you also have a chance to help a lot of people and make a lot of friends along the way.

About Me

When I was growing up it was my dream to become a professional athlete. I had two brothers and with three boys in the house, our parents signed us up for every sport under the sun to keep us busy. I absolutely loved playing sports, but I learned at a young age that my average size and athletic ability probably wasn't going to allow me to go pro at anything. I was about 10 years old when the movie Jerry Maguire came out in the mid-90's, and immediately I decided that I wanted to be a sports agent like Jerry. And flash forward 25 years to today, I didn't actually end up becoming an agent, but I've had a very successful career in sales in the sports & entertainment industry for 14 years. During that time, I've generated tens of millions of dollars of sales in the NCAA, NBA, MLS, NHL, and NFL.

In my opinion, the sports industry is one of the toughest industries to sell in. It is extremely challenging for a couple of reasons. First, you're selling something that no one truly needs. In our industry, we sell tickets, corporate suites, and advertising/sponsorship packages to companies. Some companies might <u>want</u> to be affiliated with their favorite sports team, but no one truly <u>needs</u> a suite or a big sign inside of a sports stadium. These things aren't essential to any business, and that's why having a meticulous sales process has been so important throughout my career. Sales is also very competitive in the sports industry because it's a "sexy" industry that a lot of people want to work in, and there are thousands of college graduates every year looking to break into the industry. Lots of kids that grow up as a die-hard fan of their hometown team want to work for them. But there are only 154 professional sports teams in the NFL, NBA, NHL, NBA, and MLS, and each one might have one or two sales openings every year if you're lucky. There are over 400 Colleges/Universities that offer a degree in Sports Management, and there are 10,000+ kids each year that graduate from those schools looking for jobs in the industry. The demand for jobs is far greater than the supply, which means you have to be on top of your game at all times or there's someone hungrier and younger waiting to take your place. Also, in sports the overall appeal of your product is largely out of your control. Many teams have mediocre records/losing records and aren't championship contenders, and most companies aren't that interested in being associated with a loser. Some teams go years, or even decades, without ever making the playoffs. But I believe all of these challenges are actually a good thing, because they forced me to develop the rock-solid sales process that I've outlined in this book.

Like most people, I started at the very bottom of my industry. But because so many people want to work in sports, the bottom of this industry is a <u>very low</u> place to be. Believe it or not, after I graduated college with great grades and a Bachelor's Degree, I started out making just $1,000/month in an entry level sales role (basically an intern) at a sports agency. The agency represented professional athletes and sports teams like the Washington Wizards, Washington Capitals, Philadelphia Eagles, and Pro Football Hall of Famer Darrell Green. But as a young guy without any experience, I wasn't doing six-figure and seven-figure sales for professional teams and famous athletes. I was selling advertising banners at community sports facilities that hosted rec basketball/football/soccer leagues. Not exactly Jerry Maguire's "Show Me the Money" career that I envisioned as a kid.

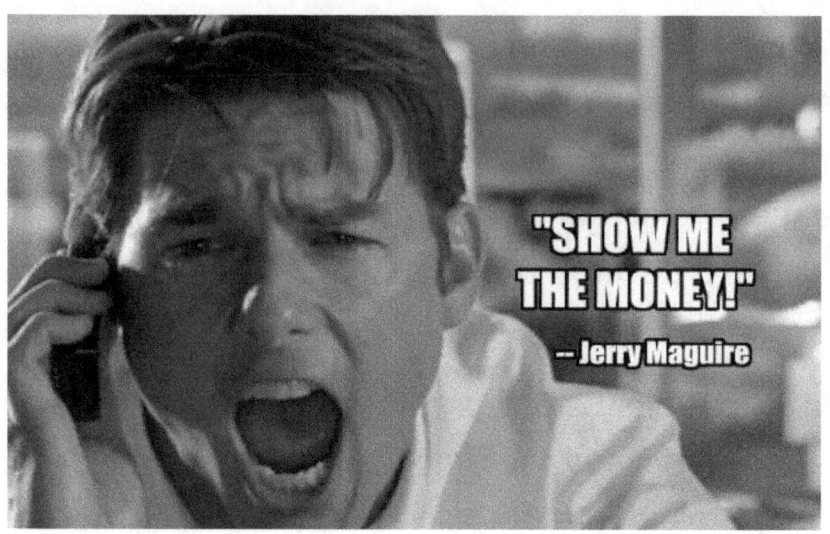

But I made hundreds of calls each week and kept grinding and hitting sales goals month after month and year after year, and eventually I got a job in college sports, and then Major League Soccer, and then bigger leagues like the NHL and the NFL. In our industry, when you work for a really bad team it makes it hard to get companies to buy your product. On a couple of different occasions, I've worked for the team with the absolute worst record in the league. I worked for the MLS team D.C. United when they won the "wooden spoon award" for being the worst team in the league. During the entire 34-game season, the team only won 3 games! A few years later, I was working for the Tampa Bay Buccaneers when they were 2-14 and dead last in the NFL. Both of those wins were on the road, so we never won a single game in front of our fans at home! People in the community called them the Suckaneers, and local companies weren't exactly jumping for joy when someone from the team cold called them. But despite all of that, I've still been able to produce at a high level consistently using the process in this book, which is why I know it works.

Attitude Comes First

The first step to becoming successful in sales is having the right attitude. You need to have what I call a "killer instinct." Great salespeople need to operate at a completely different level from people that work in other professions. Other professions don't have to worry if they sink or swim. One of my favorite books is Tim Grover's "Relentless: From Good to Great to Unstoppable." Tim trained Michael Jordan, Kobe Bryant, Dwayne Wade, and other elite NBA athletes for many years. In the book, Tim calls the best athletes that he's worked with "cleaners." I can't remember why he chose that term, but cleaners are relentless, they're never satisfied, and they have an insatiable drive to become the best. A cleaner might win the NBA championship one night, but he will be back in the gym early the next morning training to try to win another one. Cleaners are obsessed with being great at their job and they never rest on their laurels. You need to become a cleaner.

If you watched ESPN's recent series "The Last Dance" about the Chicago Bulls and their six NBA Championships in the 1980's and 1990's, you'll see that Michael Jordan was the epitome of a cleaner.

Jordan didn't drink or smoke (for most of his basketball career), because all he wanted to do was win. After he broke his foot during the 1985 season, the Bulls limited him to 7 minutes per half to reduce the risk of reinjuring his foot, and he could barely sit still while he was stuck on the bench. He lobbied his coach over and over again on the bench to let him play more because he felt like an animal in a cage. Jordan was furious every time his coach pulled him from the game after his 7 minutes ran out. He didn't care if he got hurt again because all he cared about was winning. That's the same attitude you need in sales. You have to be extremely driven and focused on your goals regardless of any setback or obstacle that's in your way.

While I don't train athletes for a living like Tim, I've been working in the sports/entertainment industry for many years. Being in this industry has allowed me to meet some extraordinary athletes and coaches. A few of them include:

- Chuck Liddell – UFC Champion/Hall of Famer
- Dwayne DeRosario – 4x MLS Champion and 7x MLS All-Star

- Gary Williams – NCAA Champion and Basketball Hall of Famer
- Gerald McCoy – 6x NFL Pro Bowler, 3x NFL All-Pro, 2x NCAA All American
- Joe Gibbs – 3x Super Bowl Champion, 2x Coach of the Year, 5x NASCAR Champion
- Kerry McCoy – 2x NCAA Wrestling Champion and 2x Olympic Medalist
- Lavonte David – NFL All Pro and 2x NCAA All America
- Marc Andre-Fleury – 3x Stanley Cup Champion and 5x NHL All Star
- Mike Evans – 3x NFL Pro Bowler
- The late Sean Taylor – 2x NFL Pro Bowler, NFL All-Pro, NCAA National Champion

I've also been lucky to work with some extremely sharp and successful business leaders throughout my career. I'm talking about the CEO's, President's, and VP's of sports teams and other Fortune 500 companies. Being around elite athletes, coaches and business leaders has allowed me to witness first-hand some of the traits that extremely successful people all seem to share.

Sales is a Contact Sport

The successful people that I have met or worked with are laser-focused on their craft. They also have a lot of energy, always looking to improve and be better than they were the day before. They're in a never-ending battle against themselves to improve. In sports, the elite players that are Cleaners don't want to just have one "good" practice. They want to have a flawless practice and make sure the guy across from them doesn't beat them in a single drill. Elite athletes do this every single day! They don't take practices off. They don't even take one play within a practice off, and they might even try to go an entire season without the guy across the line beating them once. Like Tim says in his book, the great ones are in the gym the morning after winning a championship trying to get better. This is the same mentality you need to have in sales, always looking for ways to sharpen your skills, being relentless every day, and never taking it easy just because you closed one deal. Keep grinding.

Most extremely successful people are also extremely optimistic and confident. This doesn't mean they are arrogant or cocky, but it means they always see the glass half full and know they are capable of greatness. Positive attitude is really important in many facets of life, but it's especially important in sales because you deal with rejection on a daily basis. Henry Ford once said, "whether you think you can, or you think you can't, you're right." Plenty of people will doubt you every day, so you absolutely cannot doubt yourself. Based on my own success rate (yours will vary), it takes me about 200 cold calls (or cold emails) to close one deal. That's 199 times that you'll fail for every time you have success! This is why a positive attitude is so important. In Chapter 2, I'll talk more about this so that you can learn to track and measure your calls and other behaviors that lead to closed deals, but the point is that you need to be confident because you might get hung up on multiple times a day and it will be hard not to be discouraged. Some days (or weeks or months) you'll feel like there's no light at the end of the tunnel, and there's no way you'll ever close another deal. You'll feel like a baseball player in a batting slump, when they say the baseball looks like it's the size of a pea. Things simply won't be going right. But it's important that you don't give up and you never lose faith. If you follow your plan (we'll discuss this more in the chapter about Sales Behaviors), you'll get back on track. The law of averages will kick in if you keep going. Even after you land a deal you can never slack off though or you'll lose momentum. Just get back to work like the Cleaner that's working hard the morning after winning that NBA title.

Successful people are usually also humble. Of course, there are outliers like Floyd Mayweather, Conor McGregor, or Rob Gronkowski. But most of the successful people that I've witnessed in both business and sports are "silent assassins" and they don't brag at all. The only thing they're concerned with is getting the job done, and they are so busy grinding that they don't have time for an ego. High-performing salespeople hold themselves to a higher standard than everyone around them, so there's no need to brag. You're just competing with yourself to be better than you were yesterday.

Sales Behaviors & Behavior Tracking

Once you have your attitude in check, now you need to learn how to do the proper behaviors that lead to succeed (and track them). If you learn to do these behaviors and track/measure them meticulously every day, you can take most of the guesswork and uncertainty out of sales, and you can reverse engineer a step-by-step plan to hit your goals based on how many activities you do each day. I believe <u>this is one of the primary "secret sauces" to sales</u>. It's hard work and it's definitely not the fun part, but it's where you plant the seeds for success. If you were one of Tim's athletes, like Jordan or Kobe, this is equal to hitting the weights and taking hundreds of jump shots in an empty gym. It's the part of the sales process that's not glamorous, and it's the easiest to skip or slack on, so in order to keep yourself honest you'll need to religiously track every single thing that you do every day. Many people don't do this, but if you do you can set yourself apart from the pack.

Here are the behaviors you need to do on a daily basis:

Outreaches

These are your "cold calls" or "cold emails," where you will reach out to the people you're trying to sell your product to. We will cover this in detail in the Outreach chapter.

Connections/Conversations

As you do sales outreach, you will start connecting with some of the people you're reaching out to. A "connection" could be a phone conversation or an email conversation with your prospect.

Meetings

As you do outreach and start making connections, you'll start to schedule and then have meetings with some of your prospects.

Pitches

Ultimately, some of the people that you meet with will want to see a proposal (while some won't), and you're going to need to pitch them your product.

Closed Deals

The last step in the process is to get a yes (or no) answer from people that you've pitched.

Let's start to break this down. In order to figure out exactly how many behaviors you need to do on a daily/weekly/monthly basis, we will start with your annual sales goal and then work backwards to figure out how many behaviors you'll need to do every day/week/month to get to your goal. I will break this down over the next couple of paragraphs.

Let's say my average deal is about $200K and my goal is to sell at least $2 Million per year. $2 Million divided by 12 months is $166,666 per month, so that's what I'm striving to sell each month. In order to be safe and give myself a little cushion (in case you have a bad month), I'm going to round up to give myself a personal goal of $200K per month, which is one deal per month based on my average deal. So how do I make sure I'm closing one deal a month?

In order to close one deal a month, I've learned over time that about 10-20% of the pitches that I make actually close. I like to be conservative here and build my plan based on a "close rate" of 10% to be safe. Based on these 10% odds, I know that I need to pitch 10 deals per month to close one… So if I'm going to pitch 10 deals a month (equal to 2-3 deals every week), how do I make sure that I have enough legitimate prospects lined up that are willing to listen to my pitch? After all, you can't just walk down the street dumping proposals on everyone's doorstep.

What you need to do next, is to use the pitch numbers from the last paragraph to figure out how many meetings you need to schedule. I have learned over time that about 50% of the companies that I meet with are a decent fit for my product. At least decent enough that they're interested in letting me pitch them/put together a formal proposal. Sometimes you'll meet with a company and you learn that they simply don't have a need or a desire for your product. Or you'll find out that the company is smaller than you anticipated and they don't have the budget to buy your product. Or maybe it isn't the right timing for them because they just got a new CEO and they're changing their entire strategy. Because all of these things can happen, I schedule 5 meetings per week in order to make sure I'll be able to pitch 2-3 deals per week (going back to the 50% mentioned at the beginning of this paragraph). This number can vary for other people/industries so you should start with 50% and then adjust your own plan as you spend more time in sales. I recommend looking back at prior weeks/months to see what your personal percentage actually is over time, and then adjusting your strategy. Now, how can you make sure that you'll have five meetings per week?

In order to have five meetings per week, you need to do the proper amount of cold outreach. I know that I'm usually able to get in touch with/have a conversation with about 20% of the people that I reach out to. But only 10% of my outreach (half of the 20% of people I connect with) actually turns into a meeting. Based on all of this, I know that if I make 10 outreaches per day, I'll connect with two people and one of them will agree to meet with me. Keep in mind, these are long-term averages over many years of working in sales... So I might make 15 or 20 or even 25 outreaches one day and have zero connections. But the next day, I might only make five outreaches and have four conversations and book two meetings. Over time things always even out.

I know I threw a lot of numbers around in this chapter, so here's a quick recap of everything we reviewed. If I make 10 outreaches a day it will lead to an average of two connections/conversations per day and one meeting scheduled. By doing that, I will have one meeting per day (five per week) and 50% of them

(2-3) each week will be interested in me pitching them my product. And I know if I'm pitching 2-3x per week which equates to about 10x per month, I know that I will close at least 10% of them (one deal per month).

You should create a chart to track these behaviors for yourself every day, and make sure you fill it in before you leave your desk and go home every night.

- Outreaches (Goal X per day)
- Connections (Goal X per day)
- Meetings Scheduled (Goal X per day)
- Meetings Held (Goal X per day)
- Pitches (Goal X per week)
- Closed Deals (Goal X per month)

At the end of each week, you can look at your chart and figure out what you didn't do enough of and need to ramp up the following week. Maybe you had more meetings than usual (two per day instead of one), but you slacked on outreaches because you were running around going to all of those meetings. The following week you can focus more on outreach and make sure you even things out. As I mentioned previously, your personal percentages will vary, but as long as you're keeping track every single day you can adjust and fine tune your spreadsheet on the fly, and over time you'll know exactly what you need to do every day to hit your goals.

Prospecting

The next question you probably want to ask is how do you figure out who to reach out to? Doing the right amount of outreach is worthless if you're calling the wrong people. In some industries, you might be provided with lead lists and you'll know exactly who to call or email every day. Or maybe you work in a business that receives tons of inbound leads. If that's how your industry works, you can skip ahead to the next chapter. Unfortunately, in my industry, we don't have these types of lists and each salesperson is ultimately responsible for figuring out who they're going to call on. When I first started my career nearly 15 years ago, we would sometimes use a phone book and simply call companies listed in the Yellow Pages. I'm not kidding. The companies with the bigger ads/listings in the Yellow Pages were considered hot leads! Times have really changed with technology, and there are better resources you can use these days.

First, you need to figure out what categories/verticals your product is a good fit for. For example, in my industry, if we have an exclusive sponsorship with Bank of America we aren't able to sell to other banks.

But we do know which categories are open so we call all the major companies in those categories. If you sell office furniture like cubicles and desks and conference tables, maybe your product is best suited for large companies that have more than a certain number of employees because larger companies need more cubicles. That's just a guess. Or if you sell medical devices, you're probably going to call certain types of doctors' offices and hospitals. If you sell sponsorship or advertising packages like I do, and your average deal is $200K per year, you probably need to target companies that earn at least $5-10M per year in revenue because most companies only spend about 5% (or less) of their total revenue on advertising. You get the point. You need to know exactly who your target customer is. You can target companies based on their category, their annual revenues, the total number of employees, or other factors.

Once you figure out who your target industries and companies are, you should prospect with a "no stone unturned" mentality. What that means is that you should always have your head on a swivel and always be looking around, researching, and thinking about who your next lead is going to be. Since I sell advertising, I keep a notepad next to my couch at home so that I can make note of any companies that I notice advertising while I'm watching TV. And when I'm driving on the highway, I always make a mental note of any new companies that are advertising on the billboards next to the highway. And every morning I read the business section of the local newspaper to find out which companies are making headlines by expanding in my city, or relocating their headquarters here. Your city might also have some form of Business Journal or Business Newspaper that you can get ahold of that lists the top companies in your market in every major industry.

Now that you have identified the companies you want to chase, you need to get in touch with them. Even if your company won't pay for it, I think LinkedIn Premium ($59/month) or LinkedIn Sales Navigator ($79/month) are essential tools for any salesperson. You should pay for a subscription out of your own pocket if needed (it will pay off big time in one deal). This will allow you to look up/research more people than you can look up with a free LinkedIn account, and will allow you to send between 15-20 InMail messages each month even if you can't find your prospects direct contact information.

I also recommend subscribing to a sales database service like ZoomInfo, Hoovers, Outreach, Lead411, Crunchbase, or Uplead to make sure you can access data on the companies you're pursuing. Similar to LinkedIn (but with more information), these databases can provide you with the names, titles, and email addresses/phone numbers for thousands of executives. If you (or your company) can't afford any of those data services, you can always try to guess someone's email address. The most common formats are first.last@company.com or firstinitiallastname@company.com. You can simply send the message and see if it goes through or not. Or if you're in doubt about the email format, you can also use a website like https://email-checker.net or www.verifyemailaddress.org and check if it's correct before sending your message, but I haven't found an email verification website that is 100% accurate. Sometimes they'll tell you an address is accurate and your message could still bounce back.

Outreach Tips

I've been in sales for many years and have worked alongside many different types of salespeople. I've worked with young ones and old ones, I've worked with men, and I've worked with women. I've worked with top producers, and I've worked with people that with weren't successful at all. Everyone has a slightly different personality style and I don't think there's a "perfect" way to do outreach, but here are some things I've learned throughout the years.

I recently read a book called "Combo Prospecting" by Tony Hughes. In the book, Tony talks about how you should look at sales like boxing. In boxing, you use both hands. One hand is your jab and the other hand is for your power punches/knockout punch. In sales, Tony says that one of your "hands" is for phone calls, and the other hand should be used for emails/social media outreach (IE – LinkedIn InMails, Facebook/Twitter messages, etc). Just like in boxing, when you combine your phone calls and your digital outreach, eventually you'll get the victory you are looking for.

Some people think that cold calling is dead because of the popularity of email/social media, but I believe it's still a very critical part of the sales process. There are studies that show that it takes somewhere between 7-10 attempts to get in touch with a prospect, so you need a balanced approach across various channels. You can't just hammer someone with emails (or calls) every day and expect success, because how annoyed would you be if the same person emailed you or called you 7x in a row?

I suggest starting out with a digital outreach first (email or LinkedIn InMail), and then following that with a phone call within 24-48 hours of sending the digital message. Some people also recommend text messages or Facebook/Twitter as part of your digital strategy, but I personally don't really use them. But maybe you prefer one of those instead of LinkedIn. After using your 1-2 punch, if you don't hear back from the digital outreach or the phone call, you can repeat the cycle a few days (or a week) later. After you've done this a few times (2-3x) without any success, you'll eventually move on and try a different person at the company or circle back to the same person in a few months. I'll discuss targeting a different person in the "Internal Champions" section below.

Digital Outreach Tips:

A quick tip on email subject lines. Practice writing attention-grabbing subject lines on a regular basis. For an example, you can read tabloids like the National Enquirer or TMZ.com, and craft your subject lines using a similar format that they use for their headlines. Notice how eye-catching and attention-grabbing they are. Here are some headlines I just found on both websites:

- Heartbreak & Horror on the Racetrack!
- All Signs Point to a Baby Bieber!
- Kirk Douglas Left $80M Fortune to Charity!
- Drew Barrymore Says She'll Never Forgive Herself for doing THIS...
- Tom Ernsting Rips Through Shirtless Yard Work!

Also, less is more when it comes to sending emails/InMails. People are busy and get hundreds of emails each day, and the last thing they want is another long email to read. When in doubt, I often refer myself to the acronym KISS, which stands for **Keep It Simple Stupid**. When crafting an email to a decision maker, you should start by doing some basic research. By doing this research, you'll find little fun facts about the company and the executives that you can mention in your outreach.

Read through the entire LinkedIn profile of the person

Read the LinkedIn profiles of as many other people in the company (especially in your targeted department) as possible. If it's huge company you will not have time to read every profile, so stick to the 2-3 key people within the department you're prospecting.

Read the target company's profile from whichever data service you are using that I mentioned in the previous chapter (ZoomInfo, Hoovers, Crunchbase, UpLead, etc.) and a few press releases/articles about them. If you don't have a data service, read through the company's Facebook page.

The research will be helpful when you're crafting your subject line. Personally, I like the subject lines below but you should have fun doing trial and error and tweaking these and coming up with your own flavor. If everyone uses the exact same subject lines, they won't work anymore.

- Congrats on _____! (if applicable per your research)
- Great job with _____! (new product or award etc.)
    - These are my favorite because people love to be congratulated
- Quick Question
    - This is my second favorite, because it's simple and it tends to work for me
- Question about _____
- Meeting Next Week
    - Seems to work well. I think busy people see this and open it because they think it may be about a meeting they forgot about with a new employee, vendor, etc.
- Your Company & Their Company OR Your Company | Their Company
- Friend of _____
    - If you share a mutual friend/connection with the person you're trying to reach, see if that person is willing to let you use their name to get in touch.
- Wow. Heard about _____! (per your research)

- - Similar to the "Congrats" subject, you'll mention something you discovered when doing your homework
- Ready to win market share from _____? (name of their competitor)
- Ready to take on _____! (name of their competitor)
  - These two are a little bolder, but certain to get their attention
- Hoping to help/Hoping we can help
- We both _____ (something in common)
  - This can be effective if you do some research and notice that you both volunteer for the same cause, both have a dog, both have the same favorite food, both go to the same church, etc.

After you have developed a killer subject line you're ready to craft your email. As I mentioned with the subject lines, your ultimate goal should be to find something unique that works for you and fits your personality. So please don't use this verbatim, but add your own flavor. This is an example of a format that I've had good success with:

Greetings Jim,

I saw (or heard about) _____ and wanted to reach out and say congrats (or hello).

I'm with _____ and we're wondering if you'd like to hear some examples of how we _____ for clients like ___ and ____ (the problem your product solves, and some of your best customers). Can we schedule time to connect?

Plus, our games are a blast and I'd love to host you & your family sometime this month (offer some sort of carrot here. If you're not in sports you could say: "Plus, I live near your office and would love to bring you a coffee from this great new spot called ____").

Warm Regards,

Keith

Cold Calling Tips:

You should be cheerful and pleasant when making calls, but don't be overly gleeful like a kid on Christmas morning. Nothing irritates me more than someone who calls me and is overly bubbly. Someone called my cell phone the other day in a very giddy tone, and right after I said hello he said "what was the best part of your day so far?" It was early in the morning, and I was having a shitty morning and was at the car repair shop, so that call didn't last very long! It struck me as very cheesy and inauthentic.

With that being said, when you're cold calling you do need to train your mind to think positively before you pick up the phone. What I mean by this is that you should tell yourself positive things like "this person definitely wants to talk to me," "I have a solution they'll be excited to hear about," and "I'm a young hard worker and I'll probably remind him of himself (or her of herself)," and other positive affirmations. Your mind is a powerful muscle and the more you tell yourself those things, the more you'll actually start to believe them and the more you'll get excited to make calls. It doesn't hurt to smile while you're calling someone either, it subliminally makes your mood a little more positive.

Also, don't be scared or nervous about cold calling! Cold calling is super low risk. What's the worst thing that can happen? The worst thing that happens is someone hangs up on you and you're back to square one. But there's a phone between you and your prospect, so you'll never get attacked or beat up for cold calling someone. It's not like you're walking into their office uninvited and they have a security detail (which I've done). Nothing can actually harm you through a phone, so just relax!

When cold calling, you will encounter lots of "gatekeepers." Gatekeepers are the receptionists and executive assistants for your decision makers. They are a roadblock and should be avoided if you can get the direct phone number for the person you're targeting, but you are inevitably going to have to deal with some gatekeepers no matter what. When you do, be pleasant and try make them smile. Try to develop rapport with them without going overboard (remember the example I mentioned about the guy who called while my car was at the shop) and taking up a ton of their time. Simple things like asking them how their day is going (or how the weather is over there) will really go a long way. Many receptionists are not very well paid and some companies don't treat their receptionists with much respect either, so being friendly goes a long way in winning them over. Here's a line I've used to disarm gatekeepers with some success: "I'm sure now is not a great time for Jim, but can you help me figure out when I might be able to catch him at his desk?" This disarms them because you're saying right away you don't expect to talk to him today, and it gives the gatekeeper the ability to feel like you value their help and they are important. It's also okay to play it dumb a little bit when you're calling into a company. Ask the gatekeeper a few questions about the company and be aloof. Make it sound like you're not the Cleaner I discussed earlier, and you're more of a rookie salesperson trying to figure things out. For example, "I'm new here and have no idea if Jim is even the right person for me to talk to, does he oversee your ____ department?"

Gatekeepers probably don't want to help a multimillion-dollar producer with an expensive car, but they'll probably empathize with a rookie that's a little lost. When I first got my dog, he had been abandoned and was a mess. Everyone wants to help a lost puppy that looks like this, right?

My dog Chase before my wife & I rescued him

Sales is a Contact Sport

If you don't reach your decision maker and you get sent to their voicemail, remember to KISS (Keep It Simple Stupid) again and that "less is more" whenever you leave a message. Your voicemails should be even shorter you're your emails. Don't spill your entire pitch on a voicemail, just tell them your name and who you work for and say there's something you'd like to connect about/have a quick talk about, and leave your number. Try to spark a little curiosity by being slightly vague.

If you do get lucky and get your decision maker on the phone, either directly or through a friendly executive assistant, you should try to disarm them right away. The best way to disarm someone when they have their guard up is to be brutally honest. It might sound weird, but it works. What I suggest here is to tell them right away something like this that most salespeople are afraid to say:

- "This is a sales call"
- "This is the dreaded sales call"
- "I'm a salesman/saleswoman for _____ (company)"
- "I have no idea if you're even the person for me to be calling about this" – back to the lost puppy

style, you say this even when you know they're the decision maker

There are many other lines that you can use that are similar to this, so think about what will be extremely honest and will catch someone off guard. After you get past that step, you have bought yourself a few more seconds. You need to ask a question right away:

"I'm Keith with _____ (your company), can I spend two quick minutes telling you why I called so we can figure out if it makes sense to discuss further?"

Assuming they say yes, you can start your mini pitch. "We help businesses _____ (whatever problems your product solves). Is that something you ever deal with?"

If they say yes to that, you say great and you ask to schedule a meeting at their convenience. If they say no, that's fine too, you respectfully thank them for their time and move on.

Another Option:

If you're not comfortable with the previous openers, you can try something like this instead:

Hi John, this is Keith with _____ (company name), did I catch you at a bad time?

Instead of asking if it's a "good time," it is better to say "bad time." What this does is catch the person off guard a little bit. Most people are more inclined to tell a stranger that they don't know no instead of yes (about anything), because our parents taught us not to talk to strangers. And they're probably not in the middle of something important if they answer their phone, so it's probably not a really bad time for them. So it's easy for someone to say "no" right away, and once you have a "no" from them it buys you a few minutes to jump into your mini pitch.

"I'm Keith with _____. We help businesses _____ and _____ (whatever problems your product solves). Is that something you ever deal with?"

If they say yes, you ask to schedule the meeting to discuss further.

Finding Internal Champions:

In many instances, you'll try and try to get in touch with the decision maker multiple times but you won't be able to. The people that control budgets at major companies are in high demand. In "Combo Prospecting," Tony compares it to dating and I agree with that. If you're a guy in a bar and you see a supermodel, how many other guys are you going to be competing with for their attention? Probably dozens and maybe hundreds. And if you're a woman and you see Channing Tatum or Tom Brady in the street, what are your odds? Probably not very good. You have to realize that there are lots of people trying to sell lots of things to your prospects. Sometimes you will have better luck going after the #2 or #3 or #4 person in command instead of the top dog. I've closed many big deals this way. Even though they don't have the power to make the final decision, they are usually easier to reach and more open to meeting with you. If you can get in touch with them and build some rapport so that they ultimately think your product will benefit their business, they'll become a "champion" and get their colleagues/bosses involved in the process. I've also made really good friends this way too, because the #2 or #3 or #4 person is usually younger (and more like you) than the decision maker. It's a backdoor way to get your foot in the door with a company when you strike out on reaching the top dog.

One Last Note:

If you get in touch with the person on the other end of the phone but they're hesitant to meet and they ask you to "send them something," what should you do? Don't do it! Unless it's your last resort, this will usually get you into sales purgatory where you'll waste time sending over your materials and then calling and emailing and most likely you'll never hear back. In some cases, it's okay to send a short email with your contact information if the prospect insists they're in a big hurry and promises to get back to you, but I would not send more than a regular email (no attachment).

Here is how I would recommend responding to that type of request:

John, no offense, but 9 times out of 10 when someone tells me send me something, it gets lost in the shuffle. Look, we all get tons of emails, and what we offer is pretty complex so it's hard to explain unless we're able to discuss face-to-face or at least over a short phone conversation. If you're too busy to schedule something I completely understand and we can go our separate ways, but there simply isn't anything I can send over.

Meeting Preparation Like a Mad Scientist

Here's another thing that I believe is one of the "secret sauces" in sales, kind of like tracking your behaviors meticulously every day. You can really set yourself apart by being on another level when you sit down and meet with a company. I don't think most salespeople put in enough time to get to know about the companies they're pitching. In order to do this, you need to learn everything you can possibly find out about the company before you meet with them. You should be like a mad scientist that's studying and trying to come up with a new chemical. You need to tirelessly read their entire website, and any other articles or financial statements that you can find. Print out the bios of all the key executives and highlight the key points. Look at the company's social media pages, and see what type of content they like to post. Print the "About Us" section of their website and highlight it, and make notes about what they care most about as a company. You should walk into your meeting with a folder (or sometimes a small binder) loaded with information. You should know if the decision maker has kids or not and if he is passionate about any charitable causes. If he has any fun facts in his bio (like if he loves pizza or coffee), you might even bring a pizza or some coffee to the meeting. If they're a public company, you should know if they had a strong last quarter or a bad quarter. Spend a few hours being a sponge, and walk into the meeting with some facts that you're curious to learn more about. If you walk right in and ask a question like this (or a few), you'll get their attention right away.

"I was reading about your company earlier and noticed _____ and _____, can you tell me more about that?

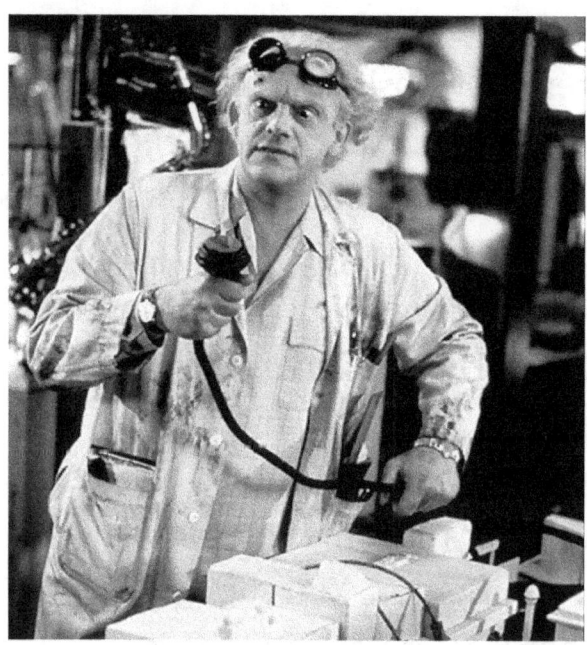

"Doc" Brown the mad scientist from Back to the Future

How to Run a Meeting

Sales meetings are all about asking questions and listening well and then (later in the process) providing solutions for your prospects based on what they tell you. Many people think sales is about using some extremely persuasive or manipulative tactics to convince someone to buy your product, but that's completely wrong. Sales is not about **fitting a square peg into a round hole!** You simply need to get in front of people, ask them the right questions, listen to their answers, and then figure out how your product can help your prospects solve problems/achieve key objectives. And sometimes you will find out that you can't help them and that's okay too. No one bats 1000 or anywhere near it.

Set the Agenda First:

The first step to running a meeting is setting the agenda for the rest of the meeting. It shows people you are a professional at your craft and you're serious about their time (and yours), and not just coming in to shoot the breeze.

Genuinely thank them for their time

After all the grinding you've done to schedule meetings as we discussed earlier in this book, you should be very thankful that they are meeting with you.

Tell them what you plan to cover

After showing appreciation, you need to tell them what you want to discuss in the meeting. I usually say something like this:

"I'd like to ask a couple of questions to learn more about your company's _____, _____, and _____ (whatever issues your product solves). I'd also like to tell you a little more about our organization, and learn more about how your budget process works and how you make decisions.

Ask them if there's anything else they want to talk about during the meeting. They might have some specific questions they want you to answer.

Set the time for the meeting:

I think this will take about 60 minutes. Are you good if we go until 4pm?

Asking Questions:

Early in my career someone told me that a salesperson is paid based on how much information they gather, not how much information they give. You have two ears and one mouth, so <u>most of your time should be spent listening instead of talking</u>. Don't focus so much on telling people how great your product is, just focus on learning more about them and their business, and soaking up everything you can in the meeting.

When you were setting the agenda, you told them you wanted to learn more about some things. Now it's time to ask those questions so that you can actually learn about those things. In my case, I told them that I want to learn more about their marketing/sales/community outreach objectives and challenges, because I sell solutions that can help them grow their brand, sell more products, and grow their presence in the community.

Before the meeting, you should prepare a list of at least six (but as many as 25+) questions that you want to ask before you attend the meeting. Rank them based on which ones are the most important to you. Not every question has to tie back to your product (marketing in my case). Some of these questions might simply come from curiosity based on the research you've done about the organization, and you think they'll make for good conversation. But your ultimate goal here is to figure out what keeps them up at night as a business, and what things are the major challenges for their business. What are they focusing on day in and day out as a company/brand? If you uncover things that they're really working hard on and struggling with as a company (and your product can help solve those things), you'll probably get the deal. People will buy the things that make their company/products more successful, profitable, popular, and effective.

Sample Questions:

- What are your corporate values?
- Or if you found values during your research reading their website, you can say "I noticed ___ and ___ are important values for your company, can you tell me more about that?"
- What is your current marketing plan/strategy?

- If you sell something that's unrelated to marketing, tailor this question to your product/solution
- What are your biggest goals for the business over the next 12 months?
- What are your biggest challenges in marketing/selling your product?
- Who are your biggest competitors?
- How do you differentiate your brand? What makes your product different from your competitors?
- What keeps you up at night about this business?
- What do you do to recruit new employees?
- How important is giving back to the community to you?
- If your brand was a person, what would it's personality be?
- What do you look for in a partner? (see what they'll expect from you)

As you're talking and they are answering questions, you will start to notice things that are really important to their business, and then you can ask for additional information:

- Can you give me another example of that?
- That's interesting, can you tell me a little more about that?
- What have you tried to do to fix it?
- If you could wave a magic wand and fix it, what would you do?
- How does that impact you?

Once you know what matters most to them and what their company is all about, and what they're struggling with, you should have a good idea if your product is going to be a good fit, and what type of solution you're going to pitch them.

Determining Budget:

Next, you need to determine if they can afford your product. Keep in mind, budget is a very sensitive subject so you may not be able to get any budget information from some prospects. When I was a kid, my parents taught me that it's not polite to talk about money. And many people were taught something similar and don't like talking about money. Also, people sometimes lie to salespeople about money because they think you're trying to somehow trick them or negotiate with them even if you aren't. Think about the last time you were in a store or shopping for a car and someone asked you what you wanted to spend. You probably had your guard up and weren't honest! But you still need to ask about budget because it helps you figure out what to pitch them (if anything).

Here are some ways to ask about budget:
- Would you mind sharing your marketing budget/budget for X?
- Usually our packages for something like this cost between $X and $Y. Is it okay if we present something in that range?
- Keep your range pretty narrow. Don't give a range from $1 to $1,000,000 or it does not help you.
- We offer three levels of packages: $100,000, $250,000, and $500,000. Is it okay if we come back to you with something in the middle tier?

- Companies in your vertical are typically spending about X with us. Is something in that range feasible?

Decision Making Process:

The last step to your meeting is to get some insight on how their company makes these types of purchasing decisions. This will provide insight and help guide you as you try to move through the decision making process. Here are some steps you can take to get into this:

Recap their biggest goals/challenges/strategies that you uncovered during the questions.

- "I learned a ton today, so thank you again for all the insight. It sounds like ____ and ____ are the things that matter most to your business, and ____ is the one that we can help with."

Recap any information you were able to glean about budget

- "Based on your feedback, we'll be putting together a solution for X dollars"

Next, you will ask them something like this:

- "How do you all go about making decisions like these? What is your process like?"

When asking how they make decisions, you are trying to answer as many of the following questions as you possibly can. You likely won't figure out every single answer, but you should pry (respectfully) to try to get as much insight as you can.

Who- Who is the primary/final decision maker, and who else contributes to the process?

What- What is their decision process like? Is it a group decision, is it a board vote, etc.

Where – Where does the decision take place? Does it take place in their weekly executives meeting every Tuesday at their office? Does it take place at their annual board meeting in Cabo? If it happens in their office, can you attend?

When- When will they be discussing this and how long will it take them to decide?

How- Is it a committee vote by the leadership team, board vote, competitive bid process?

Closing the Meeting:

Thank them for their time, wrap up any loose ends/small talk, and ask if you can get the next meeting on the books before you leave. This is a key step to make sure that you'll definitely see them again, and you won't waste time calling and calling trying to reconnect and schedule your pitch meeting. You worked really hard to get this far, so don't fall off the train now.

Pitching & Following Up

Using all of the insight and information that you gathered with your questions in the meeting, you should have gone back to your office and reviewed your notes, and put together a package/solution for them based everything you learned. Now it's time to go back for your second meeting and make your pitch.

There are three steps to pitching:

The first step is for you to review the things you learned in your discovery meeting.

- "Last time we got together, we spoke about ____ and ____ being big challenges/goals/objectives/etc. for your company. We also discussed a budget range between A and B, and the way your board votes every quarter to make these decisions.

The next step is to go through your pitch and explain how it solves their challenges/goals.

- "Based on all of that, my team and I put together this package that I'd like to share with you that we think can solve ____ and ____ within that budget range."

Then you'll review your proposal at this point.

Lastly, you will need to ask for feedback and see what your odds are, and determine next steps. I would recommend one of the following.

- "From a scale of 1-10, how well does this proposal fit into your business, with 1 being we did an awful job and 10 being a done deal?
- Or something simpler like "How did we do?"

I love the 1-10 question because if they say you're not a 10, you can respond with "what can we do to get to a 10?" Sometimes that opens the door to start negotiating some changes. And if they said 10, you can ask if they're ready to start drafting the purchase order/contract to move forward with the deal. You should also ask when you can follow up with them to check and see how their decision-making process is going. Try something like this (making it relevant to the decision making information you previously gleaned):

- "Based on what you told me in our last meeting, I'm sure you'll be running this past your board/management team/etc. at your quarterly board retreat in 2 weeks in Cabo. Is it okay if we schedule a time to chat on X date and Y time so that I can hear what the board said?"

You'll notice that I asked to schedule a follow-up call on a specific date and time. This is the same approach that we took when wrapping up our first meeting with the prospect. It's important to always try and schedule your next conversation at every step of the process. People are busy and hard to pin down. Sometimes my own friends or family members call me and it takes me a few days to get back to them. You spent enough hard work engaging with your prospects the first time around, so you don't want to have to start chasing them all over again to schedule a 2nd or 3rd conversation. This makes sure you're never in sales purgatory, they aren't going to ghost you and you aren't going to waste all of your time chasing them (dealing with the receptionist again, leaving voicemails etc.) trying to figure out if they want to see you/talk to you again.

Conclusion:

I hope you enjoyed this book and it leads to a very successful, happy, and lucrative sales career for you. By following these steps, I have been able to take most of the guesswork out of sales and have been able to consistently hit goals and produce revenue, regardless of the role, company, product, or market I was selling. As I discussed earlier in this book, I've even been able to close deals for losing teams that were really bad, sometimes even teams with the worst record in the league. To recap, here are the steps you should take to become a successful salesperson:

Developing your attitude (like a Cleaner)

Doing the proper behaviors, and tracking them every single day/week/month

Prospecting

Developing your email and phone outreach skills like a one-two punch

Preparing for meetings like a mad scientist

Running meetings and asking the right questions

Pitching & following up

I am confident that following this process will help you succeed even if you don't have the hottest product to sell. It's worked for me for many years and it can work for you. If you have any questions about this book or you would like coaching or additional help with your sales strategies, please feel free to contact me at KeithBaulsir@yahoo.com.

www.ingramcontent.com/pod-product-compliance
Lightning Source LLC
Chambersburg PA
CBHW070851220526
45466CB00005B/1954